Published in the UK in 1994 by
Schofield & Sims Limited, Huddersfield, England.

0 7217 5000 1

Insects

Schofield & Sims Limited Huddersfield.

Insects

Insects have six legs. Their bodies are made up of three parts – the head, the thorax, or chest, and the abdomen.

There are over a million types of insect living in the world.

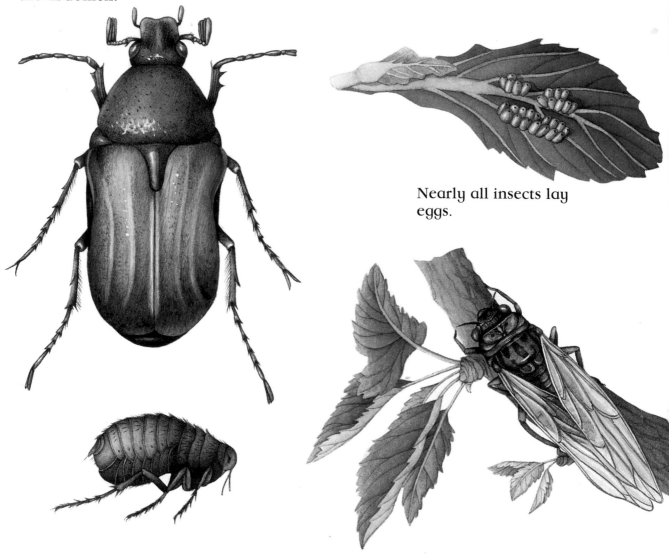

Nearly all insects lay eggs.

Certain insects, such as the flea and the louse, have no wings.

Some insects, such as the cricket and the cicada, make a noise with their wings.

The glow-worm
and the firefly
glow in the dark.

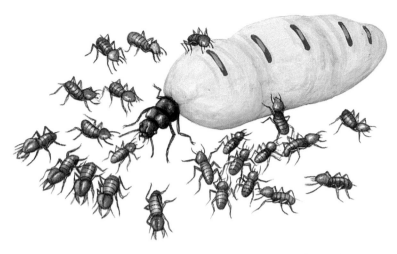

Certain insects, such as bees,
wasps, ants and termites,
live in a *colony*.

Some insects can be a *pest*, like the
Colorado beetle which attacks
potatoes or the phylloxera which
destroys the grapevine.

Some insects are useful to
people – the bee makes
honey and beeswax, and
the silkworm produces silk.

3

The Bee

The bee's egg hatches
into a larva without wings
or legs. The larva grows
very quickly.

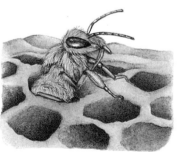

It becomes a pupa.
Its body changes, and
its wings and legs start
to develop.

4

Unlike a lot of other animals, the bee can recognise the colour of flowers because of its amazing eyes. Its antennae enable it to hear, to feel and to smell. Indeed, it is by scent that the bee identifies its friends and recognises its enemies.

The bee sucks *nectar* from flowers to make honey. It carries pollen on its back legs.

Bees start to 'dance' when they want to communicate – for example, when a lot of nectar has been found.

The Hive

Bees live in colonies in a hive made of beeswax and built in the hollow of a tree or a rock. There, they produce the honey that people have always collected.

There are three types of bee: queen, worker (female) and drone (male). The queen is the only bee that lays eggs – she produces nearly 2000 eggs a day.

At the end of spring, the queen leaves with the workers to set up another hive somewhere else.

Each worker has a job to do according to its age. Young worker bees clean the hive. Then they look after the larvae which they feed with a special liquid. Some workers collect pollen and nectar to store over the winter. Others guard the hive entrance.

The Wasp

The wasp is very much like the bee, but its abdomen is striped yellow and black. It lives in *colonies* made up of workers, one queen and males whose lives are very short. In winter, all wasps die except for some queens who make new families in the spring.

In spring, the queen makes a nest in the shape of a ball. The nest is made out of chewed wood.

The wasp's nest is made in a hollow in the earth or in a tree. It can also hang from a branch.

The female wasp has a poisonous sting which can kill a very small animal and is painful to humans.

The hornet is a large wasp. It can measure up to 3 cm long and is very dangerous.

The Ant

Ants eat plant leaves, fungus – and other insects.

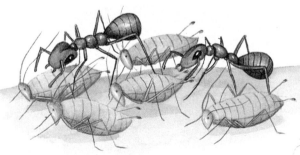

Ants keep greenfly because they produce a sweet liquid that the ants love.

Ants live in an anthill. Like bees, they undergo a *metamorphosis*. They start off as larvae, then turn into pupae before becoming adult. Ant society is made up of males, females and workers who go out to hunt for food.

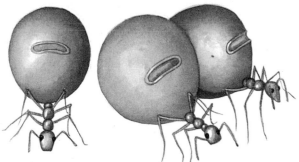

Honey ants can inflate themselves and store reserves of honey for when food is scarce.

Soldier ants form into huge columns that can eat anything in their way.

The Fly

The fly has two wings, a head with short antennae, big brown eyes and a trumpet-shaped mouth that enables it to suck food.

When the tsetse fly bites a human being, it can cause sleeping sickness.

A fly can walk upside down because it has suckers on its feet.

The Mosquito

Mosquitoes are small insects but their bites are painful. They lay their eggs in swamps and marshland.

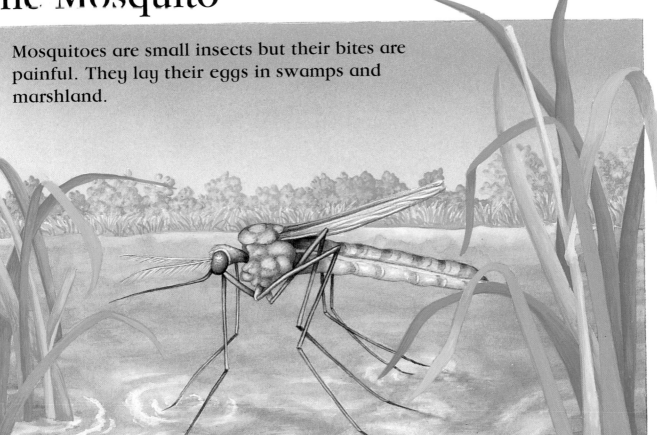

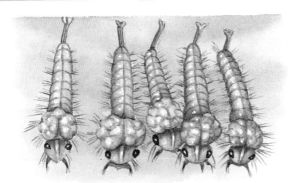

Mosquito larvae live just below the surface of the water until their *metamorphosis*.

Only the female bites. She sucks the blood of animals and humans.

The Ladybird

The ladybird lives in woods, fields, parks and gardens. It can be found even in winter in dead leaves and undergrowth. It is very useful because it eats greenfly and other *pests* which destroy plants.

The ladybird has wing covers which are hard and can be coloured red, yellow or black.

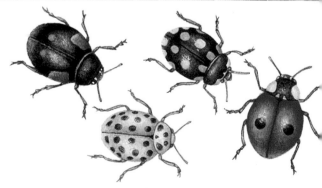

The number of spots on a ladybird depends on what kind it is. The most common has seven spots.

The female ladybird lays its eggs on the leaves of plants that are covered in greenfly.

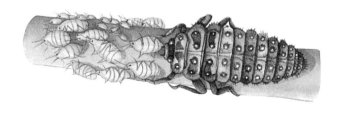

When it hatches, the ladybird larva eats a lot of greenfly – as many as 300 per day.

The Cockchafer Beetle

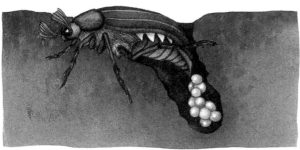

The female cockchafer lays about 100 eggs, up to 5 cm under the earth.

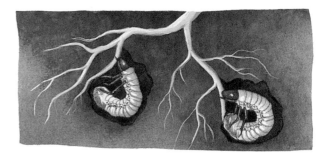

A month later, tiny white larvae emerge. At first, the larvae are blind.

The cockchafer is a small creature, 2 to 3 cm in length, that can be seen flying in the spring. Its feet have sharp little claws. It is a *pest* because it eats buds and the leaves of oak trees.

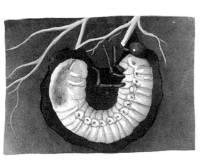
The larvae remain underground for about three years, feeding on plant roots.

Then the *metamorphosis* starts. It lasts two months.

The fully-grown beetle emerges and flies towards woodland.

The Grasshopper

The grasshopper has back legs that are longer and stronger than its front legs. This helps it to jump better. The green grasshopper can measure up to 7 cm and is most at home in the countryside. Its colour allows it to hide in grass and underneath leaves.

The grasshopper eats insects, particularly butterflies, which it hunts at night.

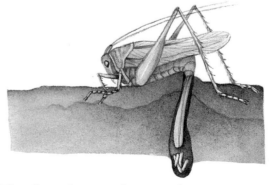

The female grasshopper has a type of tube at the end of her body through which she lays her eggs.

Grasshoppers rub their two wings together to make a loud noise.

Locusts, relatives of the grasshopper, are a terrible *pest* because they swarm in their millions and devour entire crops.

The Dragonfly

The dragonfly lives near rivers and ponds.
It has huge eyes and transparent lace-like
wings which allow it to fly quickly and
silently.

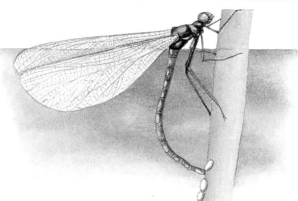

The dragonfly lays its eggs in the
water, on the stems of water plants.

The larva which hatches is very
greedy. It eats tadpoles and tiny fish.

The young dragonfly sheds its skin many times before reaching adulthood.

The adult dragonfly catches and eats insects while it is flying.

The Caterpillar

The caterpillar usually hatches from the butterfly's egg. Its head has small eyes and a mouth with sharp teeth that chew up food. It has eight pairs of legs underneath its body. It makes a silk *cocoon* using its saliva.

The caterpillar eats leaves, roots and seeds as well as fruit and vegetables.

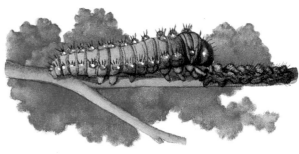

While the caterpillar is growing, it sheds its skin and sometimes eats it.

The caterpillar of the stick insect imitates a twig to disguise itself from birds that like to eat it.

When the caterpillar is ready to transform, it wraps itself in a *chrysalis*. From this, a butterfly will emerge.

The Butterfly

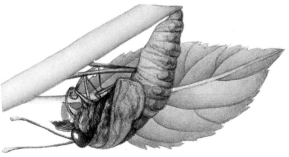

When the butterfly emerges from its *chrysalis*, it has to let its wings dry before it can fly.

The butterfly has a long, thin, trumpet-like mouth which it uses to find *nectar* at the heart of flowers.

There are thousands of different types of butterfly in the world. Some fly only in daylight, others only at night. They can be very small or can measure up to 30 cm. They can live just a few hours or up to several months.

The *nocturnal* butterflies, called moths, are usually coloured less brightly than the daytime ones. They are attracted by light. Some have 'eyes' on their wings to frighten enemies, others resemble leaves.

Glossary

Chrysalis
The stage before a butterfly when the insect is wrapped in a type of bag.

Cocoon
A silky bag which surrounds some insects, especially the caterpillar.

Colony
A group of animals, plants, etc., living close together.

Metamorphosis
Complete change from one form into another, e.g. a caterpillar into a butterfly.

Nectar
Liquid food extracted from the heart of a flower.

Nocturnal
Active at night. Some birds, such as owls, are nocturnal.

Pest
A creature, usually an insect, that destroys things, e.g. the Colorado beetle that destroys potato crops.